# MATTER

A Buddy Book

by

Julie Murray

## ABDO
### Publishing Company

## VISIT US AT
www.abdopublishing.com

Published by ABDO Publishing Company, 4940 Viking Drive, Edina, Minnesota 55435.

Copyright © 2007 by Abdo Consulting Group, Inc. International copyrights reserved in all countries. No part of this book may be reproduced in any form without written permission from the publisher. Buddy Books™ is a trademark and logo of ABDO Publishing Company.

Printed in the United States.

Series Coordinator: Sarah Tieck
Contributing Editor: Michael P. Goecke
Graphic Design: Maria Hosley
Cover Photograph: Photos.com
Interior Photographs/Illustrations: Clipart.com, Fotosearch, Media Bakery, Photos.com

## Library of Congress Cataloging-in-Publication Data

Murray, Julie, 1969–
    Matter / Julie Murray.
        p. cm. — (First science)
    Includes bibliographical references and index.
    ISBN-13: 978-1-59679-828-1
    ISBN-10: 1-59679-828-9
    1. Matter—Juvenile literature. I. Title. II. Series: Murray, Julie, 1969- First science.

QC173.16.M87 2007
530—dc22
                                                                2006013330

# TABLE OF CONTENTS

# A MATTER OF FACT

Matter is a big part of everyday life. Matter is what things are made of.

It is easy to see matter in action in many places. Just look around! People are matter. Grass is matter. The moon is matter, too.

Everything in the world is made up of matter.

# THE SCIENCE OF MATTER

Everything on Earth is matter. Matter comes in many different forms. Every form of matter has inertia. Inertia refers to an object's **resistance** to changes in motion.

Inertia can be **measured**. The measurement of inertia is called mass. Mass also refers to the amount of matter that an object has. Sometimes, people refer to an object's mass as its weight.

Some objects have a lot of inertia.

Objects with a large mass are more **resistant** to moving. Objects with a smaller mass are less resistant and easier to move.

# WHAT MAKES MATTER?

All forms of matter are made up of atoms. Atoms are very small. Each atom has a nucleus at its center.

The nucleus is made up of **protons** and **neutrons**. **Electrons** swirl around the nucleus.

The nucleus is positively charged, and the electrons are negatively charged. So, the nucleus and the electrons are attracted to each other. This helps hold the atom together.

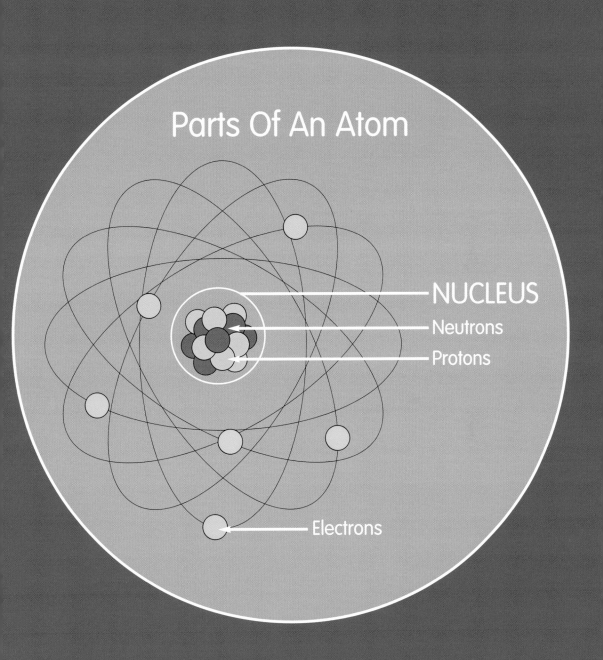

Parts Of An Atom

NUCLEUS
Neutrons
Protons
Electrons

Not even this microscope is stron[g] enough to see a single atom.

Different kinds of atoms can join together. This is called linking. When atoms link, they form bonds and change. This is the beginning of matter.

**Energy** can be used to make new matter. Matter can also be changed into energy.

# HOW MATTER WORKS

Matter can exist in different forms. There are three main states of matter. These are liquid, solid, and gas. Matter can change between these different forms.

Water in a glass is an example of matter in liquid form. Liquids move freely.

When water is poured into a glass, it takes the shape of that glass.

Ice is water in a solid state. People play hockey on ice.

When water freezes, it becomes a solid. Ice is water in solid form. Solids have a shape of their own.

When water is heated to boiling, it becomes a gas. Steam is an example of water in gas form. Like liquids, gases also move freely. They can expand to fit into a large space. Gases can also shrink to fit a smaller space.

A pot of boiling water makes steam.

Scales help us **measure** how much matter makes up our bodies. This measurement is called mass. When you step on a scale, you can see how much you weigh. This is usually measured in pounds or kilograms.

Scales measure weight.

A scale measures a person's mass. Mass is the amount of matter a person or an object has.

# A MATTER OF HISTORY

Through the years, many scientists have tried to understand the science of matter.

Aristotle was a famous philosopher in the 300s BC. He wrote about how objects are made up of matter.

Since that time, many people have studied matter. They've made important discoveries about it. Still, most agree there is more to learn about the science of matter.

Aristotle was a philosopher. Philosophers study knowledge, morals, and the meaning of life.

# MATTER IN THE WORLD TODAY

Matter is part of everything in the world. All things are made of matter. If there was no matter, the world would be a very different place.

Without matter, people wouldn't exist. Without matter, the Earth wouldn't exist. Nothing would exist without matter.

Matter is an important part of everyday life.

The world as we know it would not exist without matter.

# IMPORTANT WORDS

**electron**  a particle in an atom's nucleus with a neutral charge.

**energy** the power of forces in nature.

**measurement**  to find out the size or amount of.

**neutron**  a particle in an atom's nucleus with a neutral charge.

**nucleus**  the center of an atom.

**proton**  a particle in an atom's nucleus with a positive charge.

**resistance**  something that works against or opposes.

# WEB SITES

To learn more about **Matter**, visit ABDO Publishing Company on the World Wide Web. Web site links about **Matter** are featured on our Book Links page. These links are routinely monitored and updated to provide the most current information available.

**www.abdopublishing.com**

# INDEX